MW00979823

Marvellous Repossessions: *The Tempest*,
Globalization, and the Waking Dream of Paradise

Marvellous Repossessions:

The Tempest, Globalization, and

the Waking Dream of Paradise

THE 2011 GARNETT SEDGEWICK

MEMORIAL LECTURE

Jonathan Gil Harris

RONSDALE PRESS
VANCOUVER

MARVELLOUS REPOSSESSIONS: *THE TEMPEST,*
GLOBALIZATION, AND THE WAKING DREAM OF PARADISE
Copyright © 2012 Jonathan Gil Harris

All rights reserved. No part of this publication may be reproduced, stored in a re-
trieval system, or transmitted, in any form or by any means, without prior written
permission of the publisher, or, in Canada, in the case of photocopying or other
reprographic copying, a licence from Access Copyright (Canadian Copyright Li-
censing Agency).

Ronsdale Press
3350 West 21st Avenue
Vancouver, B.C., Canada
V6S 1G7

Set in Minion: 11 on 15
Typesetting: Julie Cochrane
Printing: Island Blue, Victoria, B.C., Canada
Cover Design: Hugh Anderson
Front Cover Art: Medieval T & O map
Back Cover Art: Detail from Theodor de Bry woodcut

Ronsdale Press wishes to thank the following for their support of its publishing
program: the Canada Council for the Arts, the Government of Canada through the
Canada Book Fund, the British Columbia Arts Council, and the Province of British
Columbia through the British Columbia Book Publishing Tax Credit program.

LIBRARY AND ARCHIVES CANADA CATALOGUING IN PUBLICATION

Harris, Jonathan Gil
  Marvellous repossessions: The tempest, globalization, and the
waking dream of paradise / Jonathan Gil Harris.

Includes bibliographical references.
Issued also in electronic format.
ISBN 978-1-55380-141-2

1. Shakespeare, William, 1564–1616. Tempest. 2. Paradise in literature.
3. Imperialism in literature. 4. Geographical discoveries in literature.
5. Globalization in literature. 6. Columbus, Christopher, ca. 1451–1506.
7. Shakespeare, William, 1564–1616. Tempest — Parodies, imitations, etc.
I. Title.
PR2833.H377 2011   822.3'3   cC2011-905740-9

ACKNOWLEDGEMENTS

My thanks to Stephen Guy-Bray, who invited me to UBC to deliver the Garnett Sedgewick Lecture; to Angela Kaija, for making my travel arrangements; to Vin Nardizzi, Patsy Badir, and Shankar Raman for their engaged feedback; to Ron Hatch, for facilitating the transition of this essay from lecture to print; to Jeffrey Cohen, for giving me the charge to write the short piece that became the germ of this essay; and to Madhavi Menon, for her astute advice.

Garnett Sedgewick was the first head of the English Department at
the University of British Columbia; he served as head from 1920 to
1948 — an astonishing twenty-eight years. The Sedgewick Lectures,
which began in 1955, honour our first head along with his legacy of
literary scholarship at UBC. They are given annually by prominent
and accomplished scholars from a variety of areas within English
studies and from a variety of locations (and occasionally from UBC
itself). Sedgewick Lecturers have included Harry Levin, Hugh Mac-
Lennan, Northrop Frye, Robert Bringhurst, Anne McClintock, and
our own William H. New.

　　The Sedgewick Lecturer for 2011 is Jonathan Gil Harris, Professor of English at George Washington University in Washington
DC. For the first Sedgewick Lecture that I had the privilege of orga-
nizing I felt it was suitable to ask a scholar who is a Shakespearean,
just as Garnett Sedgewick himself was.

　　Originally from New Zealand, Dr. Harris did his doctorate at
the University of Sussex in the United Kingdom. He is the author of
four monographs — most recently, *Shakespeare and Literary Theory*
(Oxford, 2010) and *Untimely Matter in the Time of Shakespeare* (Pennsylvania, 2009). Both these monographs have already been pro-
foundly influential within Renaissance studies. Dr. Harris has edited
and co-edited collections and written many articles and book chapters. He is also the associate editor of *Shakespeare Quarterly*.

　　For almost twenty years, Dr. Harris has extended our sense of
the ways in which Shakespeare (and Renaissance literature more gen-
erally) means. He combines a profound erudition with an enviable
grasp of continental philosophy and literary theory. Throughout his
writing he has demonstrated that historicism and theory cannot

only coexist, but even that they can inform each other and make each other stronger.

Dr. Harris's specific topics have ranged from sexuality to disease to theatre history and much else as well. His most recent work could be said to concentrate on things out of place — in space or in time or both. This concentration has led him to make important contributions to queer theory and to post-colonial theory; in particular he has worked on "Indianness" in Renaissance literature, a topic that is the subject of his next and eagerly-awaited monograph.

In his Sedgewick Lecture, Dr. Harris looked at *The Tempest* through the lens of Renaissance ideas about both the nature and the location of paradise. Taking one of Shakespeare's best-known plays, Dr. Harris produces a discussion that is utterly fresh and innovative. We thought we knew *The Tempest*, especially from the point of view of post-colonial studies. In this lecture, as in so much of his work, Dr. Harris demonstrates how much we have to learn.

— Stephen Guy-Bray,
Professor and Head

MARVELLOUS REPOSSESSIONS: *THE TEMPEST,* GLOBALIZATION, AND THE WAKING DREAM OF PARADISE

What's past is prologue. This much-cited aphorism, spoken by Antonio in *The Tempest* (2.1.261),[1] has become a pithy manifesto for teleological time. That is to say, it would seem to license a belief in orderly progress — even in manifest destiny. Little wonder that the quotation (emended to remove Antonio's suspiciously informal contraction) is engraved on the wall of the National Archives Building in Washington, DC. There, the phrase functions as justification for a patriotic version of what Jacques Derrida calls archive fever — the documents of the USA's past are sacralized as prophesies of its exceptional present and future. As Derrida argues, the archive "is a question of the future, the question of the future itself, the question of a response, of a promise and of a responsibility for tomorrow. The archive: if we want to know what that will have meant, we will only know in times to come."[2] In this sense, the archive performs a version of the logic of typology. Christian interpretive tradition treats Old Testament events, people, and physical things as foreshadowing their corresponding antitypes in the life of Christ, the history of the Church, and the soul of the individual Christian. Events before the time of Christ thus find their meaning and fulfillment in the Christian future. As St. Augustine puts it, "In the Old Testament the New lies hid; in the New Testament the meaning of the Old becomes clear."[3] On the wall of the National Archives Building, Antonio's

---

[1] All references to Shakespeare's texts are to *The Riverside Shakespeare*, ed. G. Blakemore Evans, 2nd ed. (Boston: Houghton Mifflin, 1997).

[2] Jacques Derrida, *Archive Fever: A Freudian Impression*, trans. Eric Prenowitz (Chicago: University of Chicago Press, 1998), p. 36.

[3] G. W. H. Lampe, "The Reasonableness of Typology," in G. W. H. Lampe and K. J. Woollcombe, *Essays on Typology* (Naperville: Alec R. Allenson, 1957), p. 13.

*Fig. 1. Exterior wall of the National Archives Building, Washington DC;
photograph by author*

remark adapts the scriptural "Old" and "New" for a seemingly secular, yet no less typological, understanding of global time. Fittingly, the words of the great playwright from the European Old World are relocated to the American New, as if constituting a veiled prophesy of the latter — a relocation that might seem to be licensed also by Antonio, for whom the past in Europe serves as prologue to an act destined to be performed in the suspiciously American terrain of Shakespeare's island.

Yet the orderly progress from past as prologue to future as prophesized triumph is unsettled by a recursiveness that haunts the project of the archive. As Derrida argues, its future-oriented temporality is subtended by "a compulsive, repetitive, and nostalgic desire . . . an irrepressible desire to return to the origin, a homesickness, a nostalgia for the return to the most archaic place of absolute commencement."[4] That is, the archive's fantasy of past as prologue

---

[4] Derrida, *Archive Fever*, p. 91.

is a dream not only of progression but also of return or recovery. Antonio's aphorism may authorize an understanding of teleological time, of moving forward to a liberating end. But what if his past is prologue not to a glorious new future but, rather, to "an archaic place of absolute commencement" that stands in for the future? As Derrida notes elsewhere, the aphorism in general occasions "an exposure to contretemps" — to temporal eddies and undertows that tug against the linear, forward flow of time.[5] And Antonio's aphorism, whether in its original context or in its subsequent appropriations, is no exception. In what follows, I consider how the drama in which Antonio's remark appears is driven by a dream in which progress is subtended by return, future by past, chronology by contretemps. The shimmering object of this dream is arguably what has made *The Tempest* so enduringly seductive, even to those who have attempted to read the play against the grain of its supposedly proto-colonialist logic. But the dream is a perilously bottomless one: even when we think we have woken from it we potentially still dream of recovering the past in the name of moving forward to the future. Let us give the temporally bivalent object of this dream a local habitation and a name: Paradise.

I

The storm of *The Tempest* is not just a disturbance in space. It is also a disturbance in time. This much is suggested by the play's title which, after all, derives from the Latin *tempus*. Shakespeare's play is obsessed with time: indeed, the word "time" appears twenty-three times in *The Tempest*. More specifically, the play is preoccupied with a certain kind of temporal anomaly, one hinted at by Prospero's well-known question to Miranda: "What seest thou else/ In the dark backward and abysm of time?" (1.1.49–50). This question, which comes but moments after the play's spectacular opening squall,

---

[5] Jacques Derrida, "Aphorism Countertime," in Derrida, *Acts of Literature*, ed. Derek Attridge (New York and London: Routledge, 1992), pp. 416–33, esp. 416.

suggests how Shakespeare's tempest is an event that ruptures the orderly lines of chronological time. Time is no longer a straight sequence but a "dark backward and abysm," a void or crack out of which an otherwise elusive past may or may not be recovered for the present and the future. We might call this recovery, which brings back to life a seemingly lost time, a renaissance. In *The Tempest*, as in so much literature of the time, this renaissance entails less the historical recovery of classical culture (a recovery that has since Jules Michelet and Jacob Burckhardt been called the Renaissance) than a more constitutive fantasy of recovery that pervades classical literature itself. As I will show, the understanding of the Renaissance as bounded historical period is proleptically shaped by a classical fantasy of reclaiming a lost wholeness that, in its repossession of the past as the future, also undoes that very boundedness. What I want to suggest is that the Renaissance dream of renaissance is equally a symptom of globalization — specifically, the "discovery" of the New World.

This claim may seem counterintuitive. After all, if early modern European globalization has a temporality, it is surely linear, not recursive. Columbus's voyages, and the subsequent histories of New World encounter, colonization, empire, and genocide that *The Tempest* is usually situated within, mark a decisive break with a European past in which the world was the flat T-and-O map of medieval theology, and the Americas still unknown. Similarly, on the shores of *The Tempest*'s island, we might glimpse the outlines of what Miranda revealingly calls a "brave new world" (5.1.183), an expanded globe that inaugurates our own. But Miranda's phrase is, of course, a misprision: as Prospero reminds us, she is referring not to the island and its inhabitants, but to European men whom she has not seen before. Her "new world" is her father's old world, a past that she and Prospero have seemingly left behind but which irrupts into her present as her future with the force of a rebirth.

Our willingness to univocally locate the island of *The Tempest* in the geographical New World is just as question-begging as

Miranda's misprision. This is not to deny that Shakespeare was influenced by travel literature about the West Indies and the Americas, as many important readings of the play from the past four decades have made abundantly clear.[6] Ariel refers to the "still-vexed Bermudas" (1.2.229); Caliban's name is a near-anagram of Cannibal, itself a reworking of Caniba, the name of a Caribbean people; Caliban refers twice to "Setebos" (1.2.373, 5.1.261), whose name is found in travel narratives as a god of the South American Patagonians; and some critics have argued that certain verbal and thematic details of the play derive from William Strachey's 1610 account of a shipwreck in the Bermudas.[7] But if we rely on such references to place the island, we ignore the play's North African coordinates. Sycorax is from Argiers or Algiers; the ship containing the Milanese and Neapolitan nobles has been blown off course from

---

[6] The "American" reading of *The Tempest* has a long history, though it has acquired near-orthodoxy in the wake of influential readings of the play's imbrications within American colonialist discourse. These include Stephen Greenblatt, "Learning to Curse: Aspects of Linguistic Colonialism in the Sixteenth Century," in Fredi Chiapelli (ed.), *First Images of America*, vol. 2 (Los Angeles: University of California Press, 1976), pp. 564–80, and reprinted in Stephen Greenblatt, *Learning to Curse: Essays in Early Modern Culture* (London: Routledge, 1990), pp. 16–39; Paul Brown, "'This thing of darkness I acknowledge mine': *The Tempest* and the Discourse of Colonialism," in Jonathan Dollimore and Alan Sinfield (eds.), *Political Shakespeare: Essays in Cultural Materialism* (Manchester: Manchester University Press, 1985), pp. 48–71; Francis Barker and Peter Hulme, "'Nymphs and reapers heavily vanish': The Discursive Con-texts of *The Tempest*," in John Drakakis, (ed.), *Alternative Shakespeares* (London: Methuen, 1985), pp. 191–205; and Peter Hulme, "Prospero and Caliban," in Hulme, *Colonial Encounters: Europe and the Native Caribbean, 1492–1797* (London: Methuen, 1986), pp. 89–136.

[7] There is by no means a critical consensus about this claim. Strachey's *A True Reportory of the Wracke and Redemption of Sir Thomas Gates, Knight* was published in London only in 1625; for it to have influenced Shakespeare, he would have had to have read it in manuscript. Several Oxfordians have questioned Shakespeare's reliance on Strachey; for a counter-critique, see Alden T. Vaughan, "William Strachey's 'True Reportory' and Shakespeare: A Closer Look at the Evidence," *Shakespeare Quarterly* 59 (2008), pp. 245–273.

Tunis.[8] But that does not mean the play is "really" set in, or adjacent to, the Muslim orient. *The Tempest* is a New World play; but fixing on a singular location for its island — one that we can locate on our modern maps — not only finesses how much early modern colonialist discourse entails, in the words of Barbara Fuchs, "a layering of referents" that include Ireland, North Africa, and Europe.[9] It also neglects the extent to which the New World of the early modern imagination is, as in Miranda's remark, a palimpsested space, riddled with the traces of the old. It is, I will argue, a location that is not singular, but polytopic and polychronic, fashioned out of the "dark backward and abysm of time."

II

The palimpsested New World typifies a Renaissance understanding of global space. This is not the synchronic, cartographical space of the modern map; it is, rather, closer to the polychronic chorographical space limned by antiquarians such as John Stow and William Camden, for whom the space of the present is always superinscribed by the traces of the past.[10] Admittedly, this polychronic con-

---

[8] These coordinates have become more apparent in recent criticism of the play influenced by work on the early modern Mediterranean and Ottoman culture: see Barbara Fuchs, "Conquering Islands: Contextualizing *The Tempest*," *Shakespeare Quarterly* 48 (1997): 45–62; Richard Wilson, "Voyage to Tunis: New History and the Old World of *The Tempest*," *English Literary History* 64 (1997): 333–57; Jerry Brotton, "'This Tunis, sir, was Carthage': Contesting Colonialism," in Ania Loomba and Martin Orkin, ed., *Post-Colonial Shakespeares* (London: Routledge, 1998), pp. 23–42; Benedict S. Robinson, "Leaving Claribel," in *Islam and Early Modern English Literature* (London and New York: Palgrave Macmillan, 2007), pp. 57–86.

[9] Fuchs, "Conquering Islands," p. 45. Paul Brown's influential reading, "'This thing of darkness I acknowledge mine,'" similarly insists on the multi-referentiality of colonialist discourse in *The Tempest*, arguing that the play's "America" is in many respects Irish.

[10] I discuss the polychronicity of John Stow's chorographical time in *Untimely Matter in the Time of Shakespeare* (Philadelphia: U Penn P, 2008), chapter three.

ception of space often apprehends such traces under the mark of their supersession. When, in *The Tempest*, Gonzalo tells the other Italian nobles that "This Tunis . . . was Carthage" (2.1.84), we are asked to work with the supersessionary temporalities of *translatio imperii*, in which Carthage is legible not only as the obliterated antecedent of modern Islamic Tunis but also as a way-station in the journey of Aeneas's lineage from Troy to Rome and thence (supposedly) to Britain.[11] But if *translatio imperii* maps the world in terms of progressive historical trajectories that irretrievably divide "new" from "old" — even if these trajectories must also preserve a record of the pasts that they cancel — early modern conceptions of polychronic global space equally view the past as a desirable destination that might be recovered for (and as) the future. This is particularly the case in the earliest travel writing about the American New World.

Columbus, of course, believed he had found not a New World but a passage to the Old Worlds of Cathay and India, and from there to the wealth of the fabled Great Khan described in medieval travel writing by Marco Polo and Sir John Mandeville. In the log for his first voyage, Columbus claimed that Cuba was "Chipangu" or Japan; when he first heard reports of what the native inhabitants called "Cubanacan," he speculated that they were referring to "el gran Can," or the Great Khan.[12] Columbus's mistake was quickly corrected, even though the indigenous peoples of the New World

---

[11] For discussions of *translatio imperii* and its relation to *The Tempest*, see Eric Cheyfitz, *The Poetics of Imperialism: Translation and Colonization from The Tempest to Tarzan* (Philadelphia: University of Pennsylvania Press, 1997) and Heather James, *Shakespeare's Troy: Drama, Politics, and the Translation of Empire* (Cambridge; Cambridge University Press, 1997), esp. pp. 189–220. For a general introduction to the concept, see Fredric P. Miller, Agnes F. Vandome, and John McBrewster (eds.), *Translatio Imperii* (Beau Bassin, Mauritius: Alphascript Publishing, 2011).

[12] Bartolomé de Las Casas wrote that "Oían Cubanacan y [. . .] entendíanlo muy al revés y aplicábanlo que hablaban del Gran Can," *Historia de las Indias*, ed. André Saint-Lu (Caracas: Biblioteca Ayacucho, 1986 [1561]), p. 229.

continued to be called Indians. But the correcting of Columbus's mistake proves Slavoj Žižek's dictum that fantasy is not punctured by the facts that would seem to contradict it.[13]

One of the most powerful fantasies driving Columbus's voyages was his conviction that the original earthly Paradise was in the east, a conviction shared by medieval T-and-O mapmakers. There are many examples of the T-and-O map, but I reproduce a generic, composite version (fig. 2). There are several things to note about this map. What might first catch our eye is the arrangement of the continents. True north is not the privileged compass point. Instead the map is oriented, quite literally, toward the orient: the map places Asia on top, above the T, with Europe and Africa at the bottom. Second, the map contains three inscriptions that suggest how the

---

[13] See Slavoj Žižek, *The Sublime Object of Ideology* (London: Verso, 1989), passim. Long after Columbus's mistake was corrected, the European palimpsesting of East and West continued. The orientalizing of the Americas persisted even when the latter had come to be understood as completely different landmasses from Asia. In his treatise on *The Origin of the Native Races of America* (1542), the Dutch writer Hugo Grotius argued that the Incan Peruvians were, in fact, "Asiatic Indians" on the basis that both "worship . . . the sun" (Hugo Grotius, *On the Origin of the Native Races of America: A Dissertation*, trans. Edmund Goldsmid [Edinburgh: privately printed, 1885], p. 19. Grotius argues that North American "Indians," however, are of Norse descent). And in his *Discovery of Guiana* (1596), Walter Ralegh references Mandeville's descriptions of oriental peoples with no heads when reporting on the supposedly headless "Ewaipanoma" peoples of Guiana (Walter Ralegh, *The Discovery of Guiana* [Whitefish, MT: Kessinger Publishing, 2004], p. 49). Perhaps Ralegh had seen a copy of Piri Re'is's famous map of the world, drawn in 1513. The map, signed by an admiral of the Turkish navy and stored in the Imperial Palace in Constantinople, was supposed to have been based on twenty maps drawn in the time of Alexander the Great. But it is hard not to see intervening influences at play in its representation of the Atlantic continents: not just recent European voyages of discovery in the American New World, but also old European tales of inhabitants of the Asian old world. In the map's version of South America, near what is now the border between Venezuela and Brazil, one can see a unicorn-like figure; and to its rear, sitting atop a mountain, is a Mandevillean headless man.

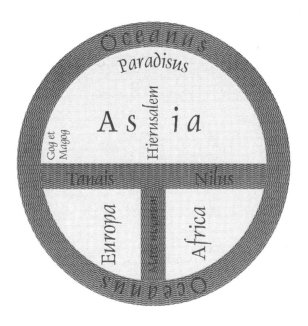

Fig. 2. Medieval T-and-O map

T-and-O mappa mundi is not simply a synchronic map of place, but also a palimpsested map of time understood, as Jerry Brotton has noted, from a "celestial" as much as a "terrestrial" perspective.[14] Right in the middle, at the intersection of the T's stalk and horizontal bar, is "Hierusalem" or Jerusalem; its location signifies its status as the world's spiritual centre in an eternal present. But as one moves up the map, one also moves back in time: "Paradisus" is at the top, suggesting that human history has undergone a quasi-gravitational fall from an orient-as-origin to a belated occident. And here we might note that "orient" and "origin" share an etymological root: both words derive from the Latin "oriri," which means to rise, to become visible, to be born, to originate. Paradise is in the orient because it

---

[14] Jerry Brotton, *Trading Territories: Mapping the Early Modern World* (Ithaca, NY: Cornell University Press, 1998), p. 29.

is the origin, the dawn of time. Even its name encodes the orient: "Paradise" derives from an ancient Persian word, *pairidaeza*, which means "walled all about."[15]

The third inscription, at the far left of the Asian hemisphere, also has a temporal dimension. "Gog et Magog" references two names that reverberate through Jewish, Christian, and Islamic scripture. In the Book of Ezekiel in the Hebrew bible, Gog is a foreign prince from the historical past, and Magog the land he comes from (Ezekiel 38–9). In the Christian Book of Revelation, Gog and Magog are equated with the "nations in the four quarters of the earth" (Revelation 20:8) — a dispersed fallen humanity in the now, awaiting redemption in an apocalyptic time to come. And in the Qu'ran, Gog and Magog (or Ya'juj and Ma'juj; Qu'ran, 18:94 and 21:96) are disbelieving tribes who will bring corruption to the world. This specifically Islamic tradition found its way into Western literature. In medieval versions of the Alexander Romance, Alexander encounters a land in northern Asia devastated by incursions from a barbarian people called Gog and Magog. To protect the land from further invasion until the end of time, he builds a huge wall between two mountains called "The Breasts of the Caucasus." Sir John Mandeville later insists that the barbarians behind the wall are the lost tribes of Israel; other medieval Christian writers fantasize that at the end of days, these captive Jews will break down Alexander's wall and storm Europe, but their defeat will lead to the restoration of Paradise.[16] In other words, the "Paradisus" and "Gog et Magog" of the T-and-O-map work to make the Asian orient a palimpsested space of the past *and* the future. Paradise is not only the location of a global beginning; it is also the name for a prophesized global end.

---

[15] The Persian *pairidaeza* was transliterated into Hebrew as *pardes*; it appears in Song of Solomon 4:13 and Ecclesiastes 2:5. It was subsequently translated into Greek as παράδειϲοϲ (paradeisos) and Latin as *paradises*.

[16] For a detailed study of the various Gog and Magog stories, see Emeri Van Donzel and Andrea Schmidt, *Gog and Magog in Early Christian and Islamic Sources* (Leiden: Brill, 2011).

The earthly Paradise as both origin and end: this bitemporality is not a feature of the description of Eden in Genesis. There, it is simply the primordial location of life, a bountiful garden of delights where, prior to Adam and Eve's fall, all needs are met. Its physical features are specified: in addition to the Tree of Life, it teems with other fruit trees as well as animals. Although Eden is not called Paradise in the Bible, it is the Eden of Genesis that informs Renaissance illustrations of Paradise, such as Louis Cranach the Elder's

Fig. 3. Louis Cranach the Elder, "Adam and Eve in Paradise" (1526)

Fig. 4. Albrecht Dürer, "Adam and Eve" (1504)

"Adam and Eve in Paradise" and Albrecht Dürer's "Adam and Eve" (figs. 3 and 4). Genesis also tells us that the Garden of Eden is watered by a river that eventually divides into four branches — the Pishon, the Gihon, the Euphrates and the Tigris — which flow through lands of gold (Genesis 2:8–16). Other references in the Old Testament further embellish the earthly Paradise's features: Ezekiel places it on "a holy mountain" (Ezekiel 28:14), where it enjoys a perpetual spring. It is arguably Ezekiel, however, who makes Paradise a sign of not just the past but also the future. In his prophesy, he gives the exiled

Jews of Babylon a vision of the restored temple that amounts to the Garden of Eden reclaimed: "there will grow all kinds of trees for food. Their leaves will not wither nor their fruit fail, but they will bear fresh fruit every month, because the water for them flows from the sanctuary. Their fruit will be for food, and their leaves for healing" (Ezekiel 47:12).[17] Ezekiel's image of Paradise as a holy mountain that will become available again in a redeemed future recurs in the apocalyptic prophesy of John, whose messianic new Jerusalem — walled by precious jewels and fed by the "river of the water of life" (John 22:1–2) — awaits the faithful at the end of days.

In its ambivalent bi-temporality as Edenic past and messianic future, the earthly Paradise of the T-and-O map haunts the dreams of medieval travel writing. Mandeville journeys east in the direction of Paradise — but for him it is simply an orientation rather than an attainable location, inasmuch as it is always separated from where he is in time as much as in space. As Mandeville notes, Paradise is too high for people to reach it, and is in any case barricaded by divine design:

> The Earthly Paradise, so men say, is the highest land on earth; it is so high it touches the sphere of the moon. For it is so high that Noah's flood could not reach it, though it covered all the rest of the earth. Paradise is encircled by a wall; but no man can say what the wall is made of. . . . The wall of Paradise stretches from the south to the north; there is no way into it open because of ever burning fire, which is the flaming sword that God set up before the entrance so that no man should enter.[18]

---

[17] For a more in-depth discussion of Ezekiel's contribution to the topography and temporality of the earthly Paradise, see Jean Delumeau, *History of Paradise: The Garden of Eden in Myth and Tradition*, trans. Matthew O'Connell (Urbana-Champaign: University of Illinois Press, 2000), esp. pp. 4–5.

[18] *The Travels of Sir John Mandeville*, trans. C. W. R. D. Moseley (Harmondsworth: Penguin, 1983), p. 184.

Instead travellers can know this unattainable earthly Paradise only in the form of its desirable material traces, conveyed from it on its rivers — medicinal substances such as the "wood called *lignum aloes*," miraculous holy water, or precious jewels.[19]

It is easy — perhaps too easy — to see Columbus's "discovery" of the New World as irrevocably altering the European geographical imagination. In a sense, of course, it did. But we also ought to keep in mind that, even as Columbus embraced the supposedly modern view that the world was spherical rather than flat, his imagination was shaped by the religious horizons of the medieval T-and-O-map. Adapting its coordinates for a Ptolemaic understanding of the world as globe, Columbus speculated during his third voyage that the world was in fact not quite round, but distended at its top:

> I have always read that the world of land and sea is spherical. All authorities and the recorded experiments of Ptolemy and the rest, based on the eclipses of the moon and other observations made from east to west, and on the height of the Pole Star made from north to south, have constantly drawn and confirmed this picture, which they held to be true. Now, as I said, I have found such great irregularities that I have come to the following conclusions concerning the world: that it is nor round as they describe it, but the shape of a pear, which is round everywhere except at the stalk, where it juts out a long way; or that it is like a round ball, on part of which is something like a woman's nipple. This point on which the protuberance stands is the highest and nearest to the sky. It lies below the Equator, and in this ocean, at the farthest point of the east, I mean by the farthest point of the east the place where all land and islands end.[20]

---

[19] *The Travels of Sir John Mandeville*, pp. 69, 83, 184.

[20] Christopher Columbus, *The Four Voyages: Being His Own Log-Book, Letters and Dispatches with Connecting Narratives*, trans. J. M. Cohen (Harmondsworth: Penguin, 1992), pp. 217–18.

Columbus specifically located the nipple-like summit of the world in an area adjacent to the Orinoco delta in what is now Venezuela and Brazil, whose flow into the Atlantic he documented on August 1, 1498. But this geographical opening up of the supposed "New World" entailed an imaginative return to the old world of the T-and-O map. As Columbus approached Trinidad, the rotation of the Pole Star gave him the impression that the fleet was climbing. The pleasingly mild climate, and the enormous flow of fresh water into sea, could have only one explanation — they had mounted toward the temperate heights of the Earthly Paradise, heights from which its four rivers ran into the sea.

Columbus spends quite some time in his logbook justifying his surmise, although his attempts to do so necessitate some creative adaptation of Scripture. First he discounts previous suggestions about the location of the earthly Paradise:

> Holy Scripture testifies that Our Lord made the earthly Paradise in which he placed the Tree of Life. From it there flowed four main rivers: the Ganges in India, the Tigris and the Euphrates in Asia, which cut through a mountain range and form Mesopotamia and flow into Persia, and the Nile, which rises into Ethiopia and flows into the sea at Alexandria. . . . I do not find and have never found any Greek or Latin writings which definitely state the worldly situation of the earthly Paradise, nor have I seen any world map which establishes its position except by deduction. Some place it at the source of the Nile in Ethiopia. But many people have travelled in these lands and found nothing in the climate or the altitude to confirm this theory. . . .[21]

The crucial words here are "climate and altitude": the Paradise for which Columbus searches is, despite his (adapted) reference to the four rivers, less the Eden of Genesis than of Ezekiel — a lofty, temperate idyll. He speculates that

---

[21] Columbus, *The Four Voyages*, pp. 220–1.

If I pass below the Equator, on reaching these higher regions I shall find a much cooler climate and a greater difference in the stars and waters. Not that I believe it possible to sail to the extreme summit or that it is covered by water, or that it is even possible to go there. For I believe the earthly Paradise lies here, which no one can enter except by God's leave. . . . I do not hold that the earthly Paradise has the form of a rugged mountain, as it is shown in pictures, but that it lies at the summit of what I have described as the stalk of a pear, and that by gradually approaching it one begins, while still at a great distance, to climb towards it.[22]

In this passage, Columbus deftly walks the tightrope between innovation and conventionality. He assigns the earthly Paradise to a new location, south of the Equator — but it still remains, in accordance with Scripture, in the orient, at least by his coordinates. And even as he refutes the received belief that Paradise is located at the summit of a mountain, he abides by broad Ezekelian guidelines — his Paradise is still at high altitude, hence its mild climate. If Columbus's America is a New World, therefore, it is more accurately a new version of the Old World imagined by Christian prophetic tradition.

In his 1885 study *Paradise Found* — in which he made the bizarre claim that the Garden of Eden was located in the North Pole — the American professor of theology and president of Boston University, William Fairfield Warren, attempted to map Columbus's pear- or breast-shaped view of the paradisal world (fig. 5).[23] But Warren's

---

[22] Columbus, *The Four Voyages*, pp. 221–2. In Richard Eden's translation of Peter Martyr's *Decades of the New World* (London, 1555), Columbus is reported to have "conjectured, that the earth is not . . . rownde after the form of an apple or a bal (as others thynke) but rather lyke a peare as it hangeth on the tree: And that *Paria* is the Region which possesseth the super-eminente or hyghest parte thereof nerest vnto heauen. In soo muche that he earnestly contendeth, the earthly Paradise to bee situate in the toppes of those three hylles, which wee sayde before, that the watche man sawe owte of the toppe castell of the shippe" (Book 6, 1st Decade, p. 32).

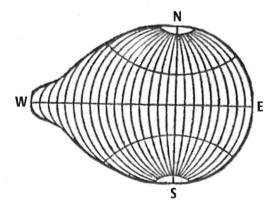

Fig. 5. *Columbus's conception of the globe, as mapped by William Fairfield Warren in* Paradise Found *(1885)*

map abides too much by the assumptions of the modern geographical imagination, and in two ways. First of all, Warren uncritically places the north at the top of Columbus's distended globe. We should, however, shift the pear-stalk protrusion marked by the "W" to the summit of the map. For Columbus clearly locates the protrusion at the top of the world:

> This confirms my belief that the world has this variation of shape I have described, and which I have described, and which lies in this hemisphere that contains the Indies and the Ocean Sea, and stretches below the Equator. This argument is greatly supported by the fact that the sun, when Our Lord made it, was at the first point of the east; in other words the first light towards it. . . . As I have said, I do not believe that anyone can ascend to the top. I do believe, however, that distant though it is, the waters may flow from there to this place which I have reached, and form this lake. All this provides great evidence of the earthly Paradise, because the situation agrees with the beliefs of those holy and wise theologians and all the signs strongly accord with this idea.[24]

[23] William Fairfield Warren, *Paradise Found: The Cradle of the Human Race at the North Pole*, 6th edition (Boston: Houghton Mifflin, 1885), p. 208.

[24] Columbus, *Four Voyages*, pp. 219, 221.

Columbus here is clearly not thinking, as Warren does, of a world with the north at its summit. Instead he abides by the religious co-ordinates of the T-and-O-map, according to which Paradise stands above the terrestrial world.

Second, Warren places the pear-like protrusion univocally in the west, inasmuch as Columbus associates it with the area adjacent to the Orinoco delta in South America. But it is clear from Columbus's description that he sees the earthly Paradise as situated not in the west but in the "farthest point of the east," adjacent to the Great Khan's territories.[25] Here, then, is my adjusted version of Warren's map (fig. 6). This adjusted version has the virtue not only of placing Paradise, as in the T-and-O map, at the summit of the world. It also, in a serendipitous fluke of typographical legerdemain, transforms the "W" of Warren's map into a Greek "E" or Epsilon. New

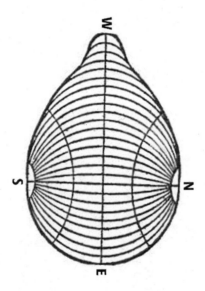

Fig. 6. Adjusted version of William Fairfield Warren's map of Columbus's conception of the globe

---

[25] Columbus, *Four Voyages*, p. 218.

World West here blurs into Old World East. Yet the latter does not entirely supersede the former; both compass points are legible in the same location. Which is to say: Columbus's world is a palimpsest, flickering between modern globe and Paradisal T-and-O map. The adjusted version of Warren's map also makes clear how Columbus's voyages west, which were supposedly voyages to the east, were fueled by a dream of travelling back in time as much as space in order to recover a lost Paradise — taking it, as it were, from the rear. Columbus's "dark and backward abysm" is, here, the occluded verso of the T-and-O map — the invisible oceanic passage that transports Columbus, Miranda-like, to a brave New World that is simultaneously an Old World.

Stephen Greenblatt attempts to capture something of the *newness* of the "New World" in his extraordinary book *Marvelous Possessions*, where he discusses the wondrous novelty of the Caribbean islands as encountered by Columbus.[26] According to Greenblatt, Columbus sought to possess the islands of the Caribbean through ritual speech acts predicated on the wonder of the New World landscape. But Columbus, like so many European travellers to the East as well as the West, was arguably motivated by a dream less of possession than of *repossession*. This dream found immediate expression in his wish for *reconquista*, for repossessing the Holy Land from the Saracens just as the Iberian peninsula had been repossessed after the Christian expulsions of Moors and Jews in 1492. The wealth of India, if not of the Great Khan, was supposed to bankroll the new *reconquista* of Jerusalem. But subtending this hope was the more radical dream of repossessing and feeding at the nipple of Paradise. Immediately prior to claiming that "Jerusalem and Mount Sion will be rebuilt by Christian hands," Columbus writes in a letter to Ferdinand and Isabella that: "Gold is most excellent. Gold constitutes treasure, and anyone who has it can do whatever he likes in the

---

[26] Stephen Greenblatt, *Marvelous Possessions: The Wonder of the New World* (Berkeley, CA: University of California Press, 1991).

world. With it he can succeed in bringing souls to Paradise."[27] Paradise here is more than a metaphor for earthly happiness. Here we might also recognize a fantasy that cross-hatches Old World with New World, orient-as-origin with west-as-destiny. And this temporal flickering of old and new Paradises is accompanied by another palimpsest. The ancient gold found in the rivers flowing from the Eden of Genesis morphs, in Columbus's remarks, into mercantile gold that is the admission fee into a Paradise regained. Gold is what has been lost; gold is what buys it back. What's past is prologue.

III

Even after Columbus's mistake was corrected, his dream of marvellous repossession was hard to wake from. Europeans repeatedly dreamed of America as Paradise. Theodor de Bry's illustration of Paradise in Thomas Harriot's *Discovery of the Newfound Land of Virginia* (1590) is a case in point (fig. 7). De Bry's illustration performs a revealing temporal compression: behind Adam and Eve, who stand on either side of the Tree of Life, can be seen presumably future generations of American householders and workers. The prophetic implication, despite the serpent's menacing presence in the tree, is that the "discovery" of Virginia amounts to a postlapsarian repossession of Paradise. But for whom? A mother and child can be glimpsed in a simple hut at the rear left: they might be a generic figure for the "curse of Eve" — the childbirth that serves as punishment for Original Sin — or they might represent a specifically Indian present and future. And to the right of the image, an ethnically indeterminate man works the land. Yet the fruits of the land in Harriot's text are not pastoral rewards for honest Indian toil: they are, rather, "marchantable commodities" that stand to make wealthy men of the English colonists.[28] The New World Paradise, it

---

[27] Columbus, *Four Voyages*, p. 300.

[28] Thomas Harriot, *Discovery of the New Found Land of Virginia* (Frankfort, 1590), p. 7.

Fig. 7. Theodor de Bry, woodcut from Thomas Harriot,
Discovery of the New Found Land of Virginia *(Frankfort, 1590)*

seems, entails less a return to a Golden Age than an Age of English Gold.

The dream of marvellous repossession did not extend only to European settlers in America.[29] In literature, the idea of Paradise was also repeatedly interarticulated with dreams of reclaiming its wealth

---

[29] See Stelio Cro, "Classical Antiquity, America, and the Myth of the Noble Savage," Wolfgang Haase and Meyer Reinhold (eds.), *The Classical Tradition and the Americas*, Vol. 1 (Berlin and New York: de Gruyter, 1993), pp. 379–418.

from oriental trade. Milton's Paradise is scented by "Sabéan odours from the spicy shore / Of Araby the blest"; to travel there, Satan must follow the path of an east-bound merchant, "Close sailing from Bengala, or the Isles / Of Ternate and Tidore, whence merchants bring / their spicy drugs."[30] Where Milton's Paradise is oriental, other early modern writers' orients are distinctly paradisal. In John Fletcher's *The Island Princess*, Don Armusia fantasizes that "Ternate and Tidore" is a "Paradice," full of "immortal fruit," "spices" (1.3.21), "gems," and "riches" (1.3.30) that are simply waiting to become European: "The very rivers as we floate along,/ Throw up their pearles . . ./ Nothing that beares a life, but brings a treasure" (1.3.27–8, 31).[31] The dream of Paradise as the end of global European venturing — the scriptural past as imperial prologue — is perhaps most insistently expressed in Luís Vaz de Camões's *Os Lusíadas*, the Portuguese epic commemorating Vasco da Gama's journey to India. The Ganges addresses Portugal's King Manuel in a dream, foretelling the future glories that await the Portuguese in an India whose waters are fed by the rivers of Paradise. This expressly biblical Paradise, moreover, is cross-hatched with another: a *locus amoenus* off the coast of India, where the Portuguese sailors are fed by Tethys and her handmaidens, who prophesize the global triumph of Portugal in Africa, Asia, and America.[32]

Here we might recognize how Renaissance mercantile dreams of the original earthly Paradise were also frequently classically inflected; repossessing Paradise for the future was commensurate with the repossession of Greek and Roman dreams of the Golden Age.[33]

---

[30] John Milton, *Paradise Lost*, ed. John Leonard (Harmondsworth: Penguin, 2003), IV.162–3, II.638–40.

[31] All references are to John Fletcher, *The Island Princess*, in Fredson Bowers (ed.), *The Dramatic Works in the Beaumont and Fletcher Canon*, 10 vols., vol. 5 (Cambridge: Cambridge University Press, 1966–96).

[32] Luís Vaz de Camões, *Os Lusíados*, Cantos IV and X; I am using Landeg White's translation, *The Lusíads* (Oxford: Oxford University Press, 2008).

[33] See Harry Levin, *The Myth of the Golden Age in the Renaissance* (Bloomington, Indiana University Press, 1969); see also Delumeau, *History of Paradise*, pp. 6–14.

Chief amongst these was Hesiod's *Works and Days*, in which Golden Age humans lived like gods, free from suffering and sorrow; the earth provided them with abundant fruits without any need for tilling the soil, and when they died they simply fell into a deep and happy sleep.[34] Hesiod's dream of the Golden Age was developed in its various Latin iterations. The Roman civil wars following Caesar's assassination inspired Horace to compose *Epode* XVI; in it he urged those who had enough courage to leave Rome and follow him in a quest for the Happy Islands, a Golden Age utopia filled with fruit, wine, and honey-bearing oak trees.[35] Ovid provided possibly the most powerful dream of the Golden Age in *The Metamorphoses*; later Christian writers found in the latter congenial echoes of the biblical Paradise, inasmuch as Ovid's Golden Age is a pastoral world "unwounded yet /By hoe or plough," at the centre of which stands "Jove's spreading tree."[36] Like the Navi tree of life in James Cameron's *Avatar*, it provides endless sustenance to the inhabitants of its unfallen world.

These classical dreams of the Golden Age are not located in the geographical orient. But they are located in another old world that, in the early modern imagination, was often mapped onto the orient — an infantile state in which the figure that Freud called His Majesty the Baby reigns supreme.[37] What links Horace's and Ovid's utopias is not just their Hesiodic abundance of food but, more

[34] Hesiod, "Hesiod's Works and Days," *The Homeric Hymns and Homerica*, ed. and trans. Hugh G. Evelyn-White, Loeb Classical Library (Cambridge, MA: Harvard UP, 1959), p. 10.

[35] Horace, *Odes and Epodes*, ed. Charles E. Bennett (New York: Allyn and Bacon, 1901), pp. 185–7.

[36] Ovid, *Metamorphoses*, trans. A. D. Melville (Oxford: Oxford University Press, 1986), p. 4.

[37] Sigmund Freud, "Creative Writers and Day-Dreaming," *Standard Edition of the Complete Works of Sigmund Freud*, ed. J. Strachey (London: Hogarth Press, 1959), vol. 9, pp. 141–53, esp. p. 150. Mary Baine Campbell develops Freud's figure of His Majesty the Baby in relation to early modern travel writing about the New World "Paradise" in *The Witness and the Other World: Exotic European Travel Writing 400–1600* (Ithaca, NY: Cornell University Press, 1988), passim.

specifically, an abundance of milk that is simply *there*, with no human labour needed to produce it. According to Horace, the goats in his Golden Age utopia "looked by themselves for the milk jars"; Ovid's Golden Age is one in which "streams of milk and springs of nectar flowed."[38] The Old World repossessed here is a phantasmatic state of infantile plentitude, where every desire leads back to and is satisfied by a milk-bearing Mother Earth. Even the archetypal classical articulation of the desire to repossess an originary wholeness — Plato's *Symposium* — points back to a lost maternal trace. Although Plato tells us that our missing other halves may be male or female, he insists that the bodily mark of the wholeness from which the gods have divorced us is the navel. For Plato, then, our desires impel us forward to our pasts.

The Paradise of Christian tradition is also associated with milk, and not just in the last lines of Coleridge's Kubla Khan: "For he on honey-dew hath fed,/ And drunk the milk of Paradise."[39] The land flowing with "milk and honey" in the Book of Exodus is the Promised Land of Israel, but the Song of Solomon associates the phrase with the metaphorical Paradise of Solomon's bride: "Honey and milk are under your tongue" (Song of Solomon 4:11).[40] This language recurs in early modern European traveller's accounts of the orient. The French physician François Bernier, who visited Kashmir in 1664, describes it as a "terrestrial paradise" flowing "in

---

[38] Hesiod, "Works and Days," p. 10; Horace, *Odes and Epodes*, p. 186; Ovid, *Metamorphoses*, p. 4.

[39] Samuel Taylor Coleridge, "Kubla Khan," in H. J. Jackson (ed.), *Samuel Taylor Coleridge: The Major Works* (Oxford: Oxford University Press, 2009), lines 53–4, p, 104.

[40] The phrase recurs in early Christian dreams of the earthly Paradise. The sermons of St. Basil the Great, from the 4th century, imagine the Garden of Eden to be not only provided with all the riches of creation but also to flow with milk and honey. And St. Ephraem the Syrian, in his *Hymns of Creation* from the same century, fantasizes the garden's fruitful soil as yielding an abundance of "wine and milk, honey and butter." See Delumeau, *History of Paradise*, p. 12.

rich exuberance with milk and honey."[41] In its early modern mercantile as much as its classical and Christian iterations, then, Paradise is a time, both past and future, of access to mother's milk. It is equally a time of maternal enclosure, in a uterine cocoon that demands of His Majesty the Baby no work, but only sleepy inertia — a state emulated by the opium-addled Coleridge in his Purchas-inspired dream of repossessing the paradisal milk of another Great Khan.[42]

The infantile dream of reconnection to the old world of the mother's nutritive body, whether to her milky breast or her womb, lurks in the Renaissance dream of marvellous repossession. The connection is suggested by Columbus's fantasy of Paradise as the nipple on a pear-shaped world; it is apparent too in Milton's description, from the perspective of Satan, of the heavenly odours wafting from the "goodly tree" in Paradise, which "more pleas'd my sense/ Than smell of sweetest fennel, or the teats/ Of ewe or goat dropping with milk at ev'n."[43] But this is a dream with a shadow. If milk signifies *both* the past *and* the future object of desire, the phantasmatic mother is not always benign: she can also become the infanticidal "suffocating mother" who for Freud fuels nightmares of being buried

[41] François Bernier, *Travels in the Mogul Empire A. D. 1656–1668*, trans. Archibald Constable (Westminster: Archibald Constable and Co., 1891), p. 396.

[42] Coleridge noted in the preface to his poem that, prior to writing "Kubla Khan," he had read the following passage from Samuel Purchas's 1614 edition of *Purchas His Pilgrimage*: "In *Xanada* did *Cublai Can* build a stately Pallace, encompassing sixteene miles of plaine ground with a wall, wherein are fertile Meddows, pleasant Springs, delightful Streames, and all sorts of beasts of chase and game, and in the midst thereof a sumptuous house of pleasure, which may be removed from place to place. Herc he doth abide in the months of June, July, and August, on the eight and twentieth day whereof, he departeth thence to another place to do sacrifice in this manner: He hath a Herd or Drove of Horses and Mares, about ten thousand, as white as snow; of the milke whereof none may taste, except he be of the blood of *Cingis Can*." See Richard Holmes, *Coleridge: Early Visions, 1772–1804* (New York: Pantheon Books, 1999), p. 163.

[43] Milton, *Paradise Lost*, IX.580–2.

alive.[44] In Julia Kristeva's *Powers of Horror*, mother's milk is not just what nourishes the child; it also blurs the boundary between self and (m)other in a register of horror.[45] The dream of marvellous repossession, then, is always potentially adjacent in fantasy to a nightmare of loss and death. *The Tempest*, I argue, not only offers powerful iterations of both dream and nightmare. It also shows how the latter is, in some ways, constitutive of the former.

IV

The dream of marvellous repossession is everywhere in *The Tempest*. It is legible in Trinculo and Caliban's tryst under the gabardine, a comic reconstitution of the originary whole body of Plato's *Symposium*. Perhaps Prospero hints at Hesiod's Golden Age too when he says that our "little life/ Is rounded with a sleep" (4.1.157–8). But it is most apparent in the relentless drive of the play's various subplots towards restoration. Prospero plots to reacquire his Milanese dukedom; Alonso longs to be reunited with his supposedly dead son; Ariel begs for the liberty he enjoyed before his confinement by Sycorax; Caliban craves a return to the island idyll that preceded his encounter with Prospero. These four characters each dream of marvellous repossession, of reacquiring a paradisal past. But the phantasmatic kernel that their dreams share is made most explicit by the boatswain. Finding the ship he had earlier taken to be lost or "split" (5.1.223) now "tight and yare and bravely rigged as when/ We first put out to sea" (5.1.224–5), he describes his miraculous experience

---

[44] Sigmund Freud discusses the nightmare of being buried alive as expressing "the phantasy . . . of intra-uterine existence" in "The Uncanny," in *Standard Edition* 17, pp. 219–52, esp. 244. The expression "suffocating mother" has been popularized by Janet Adelman; see *Suffocating Mothers: Fantasies of Maternal Origin in Shakespeare's Plays*, Hamlet *to* The Tempest (London and New York: Routledge, 1992).

[45] Julia Kristeva, *Powers of Horror: An Essay on Abjection*, trans. Leon S. Roudiez (New York: Columbia University Press, 1983), esp. pp. 2–3.

of repossessing the lost vessel *in its pristine original condition* as one that would happen "even in a dream" (5.1.239).

Yet the exemplary object of the Renaissance dream of marvellous repossession is mentioned only once in the play. Once Prospero has agreed to Ferdinand's marriage to Miranda, Ferdinand exclaims:

> ... Let me live here ever!
> So rare a wondered father and a wise
> Makes this place paradise.
>
> (4.1. 122–4)

Ferdinand notably identifies Paradise here not with milky maternity, but with a wise father. But this literally re-patriated Paradise serves as a screen for another, more maternal version. Ferdinand's words come immediately after the hymeneal masque Prospero has staged for him and Miranda. It depicts an all-female pantheon — Ceres, Juno, and Iris — who conjure a Golden Age-like world of fertile abundance:

IRIS

> Ceres, most bounteous lady, thy rich leas
> Of wheat, rye, barley, vetches, oats, and peas ...
> ... the Queen o'th'Sky,
> Whose wat'ry arch and messenger am I,
> Bids thee leave these, and with her sovereign grace
> Here on this grass-plot, in this very place.
> To come and sport. ...

CERES

> ... Why hath thy queen
> Summoned me hither to this short-grassed green?

JUNO

> ... How does my bounteous sister? Go with me
> To bless this twain, that they may prosperous be,
> And honoured in their issue. ...

CERES

> Earth's increase, and foison plenty,
> Barns and garners never empty,

Vines with clust'ring branches growing,
Plants with goodly burden bowing;
Spring come to you at the farthest,
In the very end of harvest,
Scarcity and want shall shun you,
Ceres' blessing so is on you.

(4.1.60-1, 70-4, 82-3, 103-5, 110-17)

Iris, Ceres and Juno evoke a vision whose "bounteous" plenty is associated with a specifically maternal fecundity ("Earth's increase, and foison plenty"). In this vision, however, the whiteness of maternal milk is exchanged for the greenness of grass, vines, and other plants, the vegetable accoutrements of the earthly paradise.

This is not the first time that the play dreams of paradisal green. Gonzalo sees a verdant lushness on the island where Antonio and Sebastian see only a barren brown:

GONZALO
How lush and lusty the grass looks! How green!

ANTONIO
The ground indeed is tawny.

SEBASTIAN
With an eye of green in't.

ANTONIO
He misses not much.

SEBASTIAN
No, he doth but mistake the truth of it totally.

(2.1.53-8)

The green that Gonzalo believes himself to see anticipates the green that Satan sees in Milton's Paradise, an "enclosure green" encircled by a "verdurous wall."[46] But Gonzalo's green is also not the green that

---

[46] Milton, *Paradise Lost*, iv.133, 143. For a suggestive discussion of Milton's green Paradise, and the larger early modern economies of colour in which it participates, see Bruce R. Smith, *The Key of Green: Passion and Perception in Renaissance Culture* (Chicago: University of Chicago Press, 1998), p. 137.

Satan sees. In *Paradise Lost*, green is the chromatic truth of a space external to its viewer. In *The Tempest*, however, as Antonio and Sebastian's wry commentary on Gonzalo makes clear, green is under dispute: it is repeatedly shown to be the colour of fantasy, a fantasy projected onto the dark surfaces of the island and the theatrical space in which the play was first performed. The repeated references in the hymeneal masque to "this" green grass-plot (4.1.73, 83) indicate that Prospero's entertainment would most likely have been performed on a green carpet. But as such, the masque's grass-plot is less the green of a Paradise regained than of a Paradise that remains in fantasy, demystified as a theatrical property rolled over the bare boards of the stage. Prospero's subsequent remark about the "baseless fabric of this vision" (4.1.151) can be taken to refer not just to the ephemerality of "cloud-capp'd towers," "gorgeous palaces," and "solemn temples" (4.1.152–3) but also to the element of fantasy materialized in the stage properties of "this insubstantial pageant faded" (4.1.155). And these properties include the paradisal green carpet of the hymeneal masque, now to be catalogued along with its actors as phantasmatic "stuff/ As dreams are made on" (4.1.156–7).

The immersion of *The Tempest*'s green-hued dream of marvellous repossession in fantasy is most evident in Gonzalo's musings about what he would do if he ruled the island. In ways that recall early European accounts of America and the Far East alike, he sees the island's abundant natural commodities as harking back to an original paradisal state:[47]

GONZALO

I'th'commonwealth I would, by contraries,
Execute all things; for no kind of traffic

---

[47] David McInnis's essay, "The Golden Man and the Golden Age: The Relationship of English Poets and the New World Reconsidered," *Early Modern Literary Studies* 13.1 (May 2007): 1.1–19 http://purl.oclc.org/emls/13-1/mcingold.htm, considers how early modern English representations of the Americas repeatedly draw on classical accounts of the golden age even as they fantasize American commodities as the source of future English wealth.

Would I admit; no name of magistrate;
Letters should not be known; riches, poverty,
And use of service, none; contract, succession,
Bourn, bound of land, tilth, vineyard, none;
No use of metal, corn, or wine, or oil;
No occupation, all men idle, all;
And women too, but innocent and pure;
No sovereignty —

SEBASTIAN   Yet he would be king on't.

ANTONIO
    The latter end of his commonwealth forgets the beginning.

GONZALO
    All things in common nature should produce
    Without sweat or endeavor: treason, felony,
    Sword, pike, knife, gun, or need of any engine,
    Would I not have; but nature should bring forth,
    Of it own kind, all foison, all abundance,
    To feed my innocent people.

SEBASTIAN
    No marrying 'mong his subjects?

ANTONIO
    None, man, all idle — whores and knaves.

GONZALO
    I would with such perfection govern, sir,
    T'excel the golden age.
                    (2.1.148-68)

Gonzalo's fantasy of the island shares much with the hymeneal masque's green vision; indeed, Gonzalo uses the same word as Ceres, "foison," to imagine its bounteousness.[48] And both fantasy and

---

[48] The term derives from the Latin "fusio," the past participle of "fundere," to pour; it suggests not just abundance, but more specifically the *liquid* abundance that we might associate with the waters/milk of Paradise.

masque are shown to be mere green dream at odds with barren reality: if the foison of Ceres is simply a stage property, the foison of Gonzalo is ruthlessly demystified by Sebastian and Antonio, who insistently point out its impossibility. What interests me, however, is how such demystification does not destroy but is in fact crucial to the power of the dream.

As many editions of the play remind us, Gonzalo's fantasy reworks Michel de Montaigne's account of Brazilian cannibal society as a resurrection of Hesiod's Golden Age.[49] What has tended to go unnoticed in critical glosses on this exchange, however, is how much it channels Ovid's account of the Golden Age. This is particularly so with Gonzalo's distinctive syntax of negation. His vision of a society with "no name of magistrate," "Letters . . . not known," "No use of metal, corn, or wine, or oil," and "No occupation" bears the telltale trace of Ovid's description of his Golden Age society:

> No punishment, they knew, no fear; they read
> No penalties engraved on plates of bronze;
> No suppliant throng with dread beheld their judge;
> No judges had they then, but lived secure.
> No pine had yet, on its high mountain felled. . . .[50]

The syntax of negation is arguably a mark of most utopias: even as they dream of wholeness, they contain the trace of the lack they would exclude. (Just think of John Lennon's *Imagine*, which asks us

---

[49] More specifically, it paraphrases a passage from John Florio's English translation of Montaigne's essays. In a powerful reading, Richard Halpern has argued that Gonzalo's reworking of Montaigne amounts to what he calls "white cannibalism": a proto-imperialist gesture that works to replace Montaigne's account of Brazil and the Tupinamba Indians with a New World peopled by Golden Age Europeans. As a result, "All explicit reference to the New World vanishes, though an implicit and ghostly reference still inheres in the Arcadian genre itself." See Halpern, "'The Picture of Nobody': White Cannibalism in *The Tempest*," in David Lee Miller and Sharon O'Dair (eds.), *The Production of English Renaissance Culture* (Ithaca, NY: Cornell University Press, 1994), pp. 262–92, esp. p. 268.
[50] Ovid, *Metamorphoses*, p. 4.

to imagine that there's "no heaven," "no religion," "no countries.") Ovid's Golden Age, like Gonzalo's, lacks the lacks of the present; one of these present lacks, of course, is the absence of freedom resulting from the subjection that is the requisite of sovereignty. Yet the freedom that is the hallmark of the Golden Age requires, as Sebastian and Antonio point out, a founding act of sovereignty to produce the illusion of no sovereignty.[51] As Antonio memorably says, "The latter end of his commonwealth forgets the beginning." The forgotten "beginning" of Paradise, in other words, is the effect of something that in fantasy is excluded from and even supposed to come after it. It is difficult not to scoff here at Gonzalo, if only because — as Heather James has argued — the traveller William Strachey's anarchic experience of shipwreck on Bermuda in 1609 had recently provided a frightening counterexample to Gonzalo's fantasy of an island with no sovereignty.[52] But surely something more complicated is going on here than simple critique: puncturing the dream of the Golden Age, as Antonio and Sebastian do, only whets desire for it further. Indeed, the loss of the dream — the experience of cruelly waking from it — is incorporated into and constitutive of the dream. This constitutive loss is, to turn Antonio's words back on him, the beginning that the latter end forgets.

And everywhere in *The Tempest*, what would seem to spell the loss of the dream only adds to its strength. As we have seen, milk is abundantly and spontaneously available in Hesiod's and Ovid's golden worlds; there are no workers needed to produce or transport it. *The Tempest* brings to visibility the labour that the fantasy of the

---

[51] I am, of course, alluding here to recent discussions of sovereignty and the exception prompted by the work of Carl Schmitt, especially his 1922 study *Political Theology: Four Chapters on the Concept of Sovereignty*, trans. George D. Schwab (Chicago: University of Chicago Press, 2004). See in particular Giorgio Agamben's *Homo Sacer: Sovereign Power and Bare Life*, trans. Daniel Heller-Roazen (Palo Alto, CA: Stanford University Press, 1998), and *State of Exception*, trans. Kevin Attell (Chicago: University of Chicago Press, 2005).

[52] James, *Shakespeare's Troy*, p. 199.

Golden Age would exclude — Caliban has to do the work of bringing the wood in, of finding food, of creating the comforts enjoyed
by Prospero and Miranda. And we might expect this visibility to
have the effect of disturbing the play's dream of Paradise and the
Golden Age, demystifying its oppressive yet disavowed conditions
of possibility. But Caliban's labour is subject to a telling displace-
ment. Ferdinand structurally takes the place of Caliban by being
made into an indentured servant who carts logs for Prospero and
Miranda; rather than destroying the dream of Paradise by making
explicit the hard labour that is necessary to produce its comforts,
however, Ferdinand's work is transformed into a test of his worthi-
ness to be admitted into what he himself terms "paradise" — a test
he passes and whose prize he embraces unconditionally. Labour here
is no longer the disavowed material precondition for a fantasy of
Paradise from which it must be excluded. Instead, it is incorporated
into the fantasy — not as that which would wake up its dreamer,
however, but rather as that which productively defers the dream
and, by deferring it, increases its allure. Indeed, deferral is the hallmark of Ferdinand's "paradise": the temporal thrust of the hymeneal masque is that marriage promises a paradise, but *not yet*.

Dreams of Paradise and the Golden Age exclude not only the
labour necessary to produce their nutritious abundance; more specifically, they erase the producers of their milk. As I have argued,
these dreams have a distinctively maternal substrate. Yet the mothers
whom we might expect to be the sources of paradisal milk are absent
— except in sublated form, as Paradise itself. Gilles Deleuze and Félix
Guattari have famously entertained the possibility of a body without organs; in Columbus's fantasy of Paradise, we get the opposite —
an organ without a body, or more specifically, a nipple without a
mother.[53] Yet Columbus's is a nipple that must, like Ferdinand's

---

[53] Gilles Deleuze and Félix Guattari, *A Thousand Plateaus: Capitalism and Schizo-
phrenia, Vol. 2*, trans. Brian Massumi (Minneapolis: University of Minnesota
Press, 1984), esp. pp. 165–84.

hymeneal Paradise, remain perpetually deferred: he moves in its direction, but he never gets to see it, let alone feed from it. The figure of the mother is evoked only metonymically, and even then her nipple remains beyond the visible horizon. Perhaps that is because the mother, as I have suggested, is in fantasy too ambivalent a figure to be fully incorporated into dreams of Paradise. Even as her milk supposedly answers His Majesty the Baby's every need, there is always the threatening possibility that this milk may prove to be either toxic or simply not forthcoming — that "foison" will shade into "poison." And any reminder of the infanticidal suffocating mother or of the bad breast that withholds rather than nourishes has the potential to make the dreamer awaken from the reverie of marvellous repossession.[54] Yet just as *The Tempest* converts potentially damaging reminders of labour into lubricants for the dream of Paradise, so does it harness the energy of the dangerous mother in a way that spurs rather than disrupts the dream.

On the one hand, as several readers of the play have noted, *The Tempest* is free of mothers except as absent presences stranded in the fog separating remembrance from oblivion — Miranda's dimly recalled mother, the long-dead Sycorax.[55] Yet as we have seen, the play draws on the resources of the nourishing mother to present its vision of paradisal "foison." More startlingly, *The Tempest* also repeatedly evokes the metaphorical attributes of the suffocating mother, and in ways that reveal the dark shadow of "poison" lurking within the verdant dream of "foison." Take the tree that presides benignly over Ovid's Golden Age. It keeps returning in *The Tempest*,

---

[54] I am alluding here to Melanie Klein's theory of infantile phantasy, according to which the mother's breast is a part object that is both a "good" provider and a "bad" withholder; see Klein, *Developments in Psycho-analysis*, ed. Joan Riviere (London: Hogarth Press, 1952).

[55] On the absence of women and mothers in *The Tempest*, see Stephen Orgel, "Prospero's Wife," *Representations* 8 (1984): 1–13; and Ann Thompson, "'Miranda, where's your sister?': Reading Shakespeare's *The Tempest*," in Susan Sellers (ed.), *Feminist Criticism: Theory and Practice* (Toronto: University of Toronto Press, 1991), pp. 45–55.

but as a nightmare figure of violent loss. Hence the oak in which Sycorax confines Ariel is a metonymy for a suffocating maternity that suggests intrauterine death rather than paradisal abundance. The tree reappears, again in nightmare form, in another speech indebted to Ovid:

> I have bedimm'd
> The noontide sun, call'd forth the mutinous winds,
> And 'twixt the green sea and the azur'd vault
> Set roaring war; to the dread rattling thunder
> Have I given fire, and rifted Jove's stout oak
> With his own bolt.
>
> (5.1.41-6)

Prospero speaks here, as many readers have noted, in the words of Ovid's oriental sorceress, Medea.[56] She is the archetype of the suffocating mother who kills rather than nourishes her children, a forerunner of that other oriental mother-witch, Sycorax, whose magical powers — mirroring Prospero/Medea's — can "control the moon, make flows and ebbs" (5.1.270). Yet Prospero's turn as Medea is, by a logic that should now seem predictable, less a challenge to the dream of a Golden Age than yet another version of it. His reference to "rift[ing] Jove's stout oak" — a daring reworking of Medea's more simple claim that "mighty oaks from out their soil I tear"[57] — evokes Ovid's pastoral image of the Golden Age presided over by "Jove's spreading tree," albeit now as an absent presence. Prospero's admission to "rifting" Jove's oak, however, is the prelude to his supposed desire for justice and reconciliation, to putting together what has been broken, to recovering something of the utopia that he has supposedly vandalized. Rather than disrupting the dream of Paradise, then, the figure of the damaging mother guarantees its status as dream, as perpetually deferred future hope of a past restored.

---

[56] For a particularly canny teasing out of the similarities between Prospero and Medea, see Orgel, "*Prospero's* Wife," 61.
[57] Ovid, *Metamorphoses*, p. 150.

For the Golden Age is never a self-identical presence; it is, rather, always already an apparition marked by lack that beckons desire for the past-as-future, as we see in Horace's hope that the Golden Age of yore might exist on some as yet undiscovered Happy Isle. Like Horace and like Columbus, Gonzalo and Prospero long to repossess a plenitude lost in the backward and dark abysm of time. Yet in *The Tempest* — as in Horace and Columbus — that plenitude must remain lost, whether as a result of Antonio and Sebastian's cruel critique of Gonzalo's dream or of Prospero's dark arts which have seemingly betrayed his dream. In other words, the dream can survive only as long as its object remains lost. What I find particularly unsettling about *The Tempest* is how thoroughly it forecloses on the possibility of resisting the dream's allure. And it does so most movingly, but also most tragically, by making its "native" islander the most eloquent spokesperson for that dream. The lineaments of a loss that is constitutive of an open-ended desire for repossession are most powerfully exposed, even as they are most seductively articulated, by Caliban. He says of his island reveries that "in dreaming/ The clouds methought would open and show riches/ Ready to drop upon me, that when I waked/ I cried to dream again" (3.2.140–3). The Golden Age can indeed be enjoyed, Caliban ambivalently reassures Stefano and Trinculo, but only as a dream. More specifically, the hope of future riches is a hope of repossession. Past is prologue.

This is why, perhaps, Prospero can claim of Caliban that "this thing of darkness I/ acknowledge mine" (5.1.275–6). No matter how much criticism of *The Tempest* has sought to distinguish the two, whether by making Prospero a spokesperson for civilization opposed to Caliban's base savagery or by siding with the latter against the former's proto-colonialist rule, each dreams in the same register. And that is the register of a globalization predicated on the reconfiguration of past plenitude as the promise of future "riches." *The Tempest*'s dreams of plenty as both prologue and prophesy might recall another Shakespearean dream of the orient. The supposedly

New World "yellow sands" (1.2.375) to which Ariel invites us in *The Tempest* uncannily parallels the Indian "yellow sands" evoked by Titania in *A Midsummer Night's Dream* (2.1.126). These Indian sands, on which a pregnant votaress sits next to Neptune's shore, point back to a maternal *locus amoenus*. But Titania's oriental beachside resort is also a paradise that points forward to a mercantile future: it is plied by traders "rich with merchandise" (2.1.134). Dreams of recovering a classical paradisal past are, in the age of globalization, readily transformed into dreams of future acquisitions. These dreams metaleptically transform their supposed end, gold, into the means by which Paradise will be bought — and, in the process, the means by which Paradise will also remain perpetually deferred. These dreams are, in other words, the engines of a futurity according to which the present seeks to progress by immersing itself in the phantasm of an ever-elusive past.

Something similar happens in *The Tempest*. Prospero wakes up from the dream of possessing the island. (And that is why the play is, in certain crucial ways, a *post*-colonialist fantasy.) But Prospero cannot wake up from the dream of *repossessing* an originary plenitude in the east. The object of this dream is given a new habitation and name — Milan — but, like Mandeville's or Columbus's or Titania's oriental paradises, it remains perpetually beyond the visible horizon. Such is the power of what we might call the play's waking dream of marvellous repossession.

V

Which makes me wonder: are anti-colonial rewritings of *The Tempest* — whether from the Caribbean, South America, Africa, Asia, or the Pacific — not just important and even politically necessary reappropriations of the play, but also repetitions of its driving fantasy? Many of these rewritings seek to reclaim an original language or identity lost in the fall occasioned by European contact; in the process, they seek to make that originary past not just pre-colonial prologue but also nativist prophesy.[58] The Uruguayan essayist José Enrique Rodó reads the airy spirit Ariel as a figure for the pure Latin American;[59] the Martiniquan poet Aimé Césaire's adaptation, *Une Tempête*, features a Caliban who represents the timeless essence of a *negritude* that will resist and outlive colonial enslavement;[60] the former British Raj civil servant Philip Mason styles Caliban as a South Asian Indian reclaiming a precolonial identity independent of a British Prospero;[61] the Rhodesian/Zimbabwean nationalist Ndabaningi Sithole sees Caliban as a true black African;[62] and the Barbadian poet Edward Kamau Brathwaite transforms Sycorax into the cybernetic representative of a native writing that precedes and survives Prospero's.[63] In every instance, the movement forward from colonialism entails a movement in fantasy, via *The Tempest*, back to the past.

In *The Political Unconscious*, Fredric Jameson argues that romance is driven by the utopian desire to move beyond seeming necessity. Indeed, Leontes's speech about his supposedly dead wife Hermione's now living statue at the conclusion of *The Winter's Tale* provides Jameson with his chapter's epigraph:

---

[58] For a thorough survey of postcolonial rewritings of *The Tempest*, including the five texts I cite here, see Chantal Zabus, *Tempests after Shakespeare* (London and New York: Palgrave Macmillan, 2002), passim.

[59] José Enrique Rodó, *Ariel*, trans. Margaret Sayers Peden (Austin, TX: University of Texas Press, 1988 [1900]).

[60] Aimé Césaire, *Une Tempête* (Paris: Editions du Seuil, 1980 [1968]).

[61] Philip Mason, "Foreword," Octave Mannoni, *Prospero and Caliban: A Study of the Psychology of Colonisation*, trans. Pamela Powesland (University of Michigan Press, 1981 [1950]), pp. 9–16.

[62] Ndabaningi Sithole, *African Nationalism* (London: Oxford University Press, 1960), pp. 165–66.

[63] Kamau Brathwaite, "Letter SycoraX," *Middle Passages* (New York: New Directions Books, 1993), pp. 95–116. Zabus discusses Brathwaite's complex engagements with *The Tempest* throughout his career — including his assertion that Sycorax's language is "mother's milk" — on pp. 58–63.

O, she's warm!
If this be magic, let it be an art
Lawful as eating.

(5.3.109-10)[64]

On the one hand, Jameson interprets Shakespearean romance as situated within historical processes of social and economic transition: a late play like *The Winter's Tale*, or even an early quasi-romance like *The Comedy of Errors*, recalls with nostalgia an old world even as it opposes "'the phantasmagoria of 'imagination' to the bustling commercial activity at work all around it."[65] Yet in Jameson's view, Leontes's remark also speaks to the utopian longing for a better world that is a defining feature not only of the genre as a whole but also of Marxism's vision of history. Far from discrediting this vision, Jameson suggests, the element of romantic utopianism helps explain Marxism's persistence and vitality. And he argues that utopian desire like Leontes's, which takes as its object a "magic" alternative to the seemingly iron-clad necessities of the current "lawful" order, is crucial to both a progressive politics and a progressive critical practice. For Jameson, then romance is the genre of subjunctive futurity, of new possibilities that critique the present. But I wonder how different his argument would be if he were to take *The Tempest* rather *The Winter's Tale* as his paradigmatic instance of romance. For the former reminds us that if romance is about futurity it is equally about repossession, about getting back what one has lost. Indeed, *The Winter's Tale* lends itself to a similar reading: the "magical" alternative to the necessity of the present amounts in this play, as in *The Tempest*, to a restoration of the past

---

[64] Fredric Jameson, *The Political Unconscious: Narrative as Socially Symbolic Act* (London and New York: Methuen, 1981), p. 103. I discuss Jameson's reading of these lines from *The Winter's Tale* in Jonathan Gil Harris, *Shakespeare and Literary Theory* (Oxford: Oxford University Press, 2010), pp. 171–72.

[65] Jameson, *The Political Unconscious*, p. 148.

as it was — Leontes reacquires the wife he thought he had lost.[66] But there is also a crucial difference. *The Winter's Tale* folds its climactic instance of marvellous repossession into its visible narrative economy: we see Hermione, then she disappears, then we see her again. *The Tempest*, by contrast, adds vitality to its dream of restoration by *withholding* from view what it longs to repossess. In the process, it implicates its spectators and readers more fully in the desire that sponsors the dream, for this dream — as I have argued — is fueled by absence. That which is lost and repossessed in *The Tempest* (family, dukedom, extra-arboreal liberty, indigenous communion with the island) is never fully present on stage, whether as past or as future. Instead, it is conjured up through acts of recollection or prophesy.

But is this not what anti-colonial rewritings of *The Tempest* also do? Even as these rewritings dissent from the play's colonialist politics, they feel compelled to repeat something in the play's structure of fantasy, something specific to the recursive temporality of romance — the dream of repossessing, in an unspecified future, a pure origin anterior to and exiled from our current regimes of representation. Is it possible to resist this dream without lending more fuel to it? Or is resistance the very stuff of which this dream is made?

One recent anti-colonial rewriting of *The Tempest* is of particular interest to me here, as it brings Paradise into sharp focus as the problematic object of the play's desire. And because of the other non-Shakespearean intertexts it engages, it also puts enormous pressure on the dream of marvellous repossession. The MAU dance and theatre company's extraordinary performance piece *Tempest without a Body* (2007), devised by the New Zealand-Samoan playwright and choreographer Lemi Ponifasio, engages *The Tempest* only in broad, mostly non-verbal, brushstrokes.[67] The program note

---

[66] I have made this argument elsewhere; see Jonathan Gil Harris, "Four Exoskeletons and No Funeral," *New Literary History* 43 (2012): forthcoming.

informs us that the piece is concerned with colonialism, terrorism, and institutional injustice post-9/11; it also invokes the ideas of Walter Benjamin and Giorgio Agamben as well as Shakespeare's play. The piece begins in darkness: suddenly we hear a deafening discordant clang, under which the sound of a muezzin calling the faithful to prayer can be heard. Slowly, a dim light illuminates a huge rectangular shape suspended in mid-air — a tower? — as the opening noise increases in intensity. The light reveals a solitary figure beneath the rectangle: it is androgynous and hunched up, and it has small, broken wings (fig. 8). The figure begins to move at high speed, with impossibly small steps, around the stage, staring up at the top of the rectangle, a sightline whose object remains invisible to the audience. As s/he moves, s/he suddenly emits a piercing scream. And then another. And then another.

As this suggests, *Tempest without a Body* reconfigures the opening storm of Shakespeare's play as the storm that blows Walter Benjamin's angel of History out of Paradise. Benjamin describes this storm in the ninth of his *Theses on the Philosophy of History*:

> A Klee painting named "Angelus Novus" shows an angel looking as though he is about to move away from something he is fixedly contemplating. His eyes are staring, his mouth is open, his wings are spread. This is how one pictures the angel of history. His face is turned toward the past. Where we perceive a chain of events, he sees one single catastrophe which keeps piling wreckage and hurls it in front of his feet. The angel would like to stay, awaken the dead, and make whole what has been smashed. But a storm is blowing in from Paradise; it has got caught in his wings with such a violence that the angel can no

---

67 *Tempest without a Body* premiered in Vienna in 2007; it has since toured the world, playing at venues such as the Queen Elizabeth Hall, London, in 2008, the Theatre de la Ville, Paris, in 2010 and the Volksbühne, Berlin, in 2010. The performance I saw was mounted at Darmouth College, Hanover New Hampshire, in April 2011.

Fig. 8. Tempest without a Body, *Lemi Ponifasio/MAU*

longer close them. The storm irresistibly propels him into the future to which his back is turned, while the pile of debris before him grows skyward. This storm is what we call progress.[68]

Benjamin's *Theses*, written at the high wind of the storm that produced fascist Germany, are devastating meditations on history and progress. But as Thesis 9 suggests, they are equally troubled meditations on Paradise and the dream of repossession. The angel desperately wishes to go back to Paradise, to restore what has been lost, to "make whole what has been smashed." But it is impossible for him to do so: there is no path back to any originary wholeness. The best that can be hoped for is what Benjamin calls, in Thesis 2, a

---

[68] Walter Benjamin, *Illuminations*, ed. Hannah Arendt (New York: Schocken Books, 1969), pp. 257–58.

"weak messianic power" — the power of the present generation to remember and redeem the oppressed of history, made invisible within homogenous narratives of progress, by fighting for a more just world *now*.[69] This power is an imperfect honouring of a subaltern past, not a return to it.

By reconfiguring Shakespeare's opening tempest as Benjamin's storm of history, *Tempest without a Body* would seem to acknowledge both the power of the desire to return to a phantasmatic Paradise and the impossibility of doing so, throwing its lot instead behind the project of redeeming the past victims of imperialist and colonialist violence by criticizing the injustices of our current moment. Much of *Tempest without a Body* is loosely allegorical; it is a meditation on expanding state powers in the wake of 9/11 and the disappearance of non-Western bodies — bodies of the present in Guantánamo prison, but also bodies of the past in white settler nations such as New Zealand. Here *Tempest without a Body* seems to derive inspiration from Agamben, particularly his discussion of the state of exception. The notion might be summed up by Antonio's remark that "the end forgets its beginning" — in this case, the "end" being the future survival of supposedly free democratic nations and the "beginning" the undemocratic violence to which these nations resort against "exceptional" bodies outside the law, reduced to bare life. In *Tempest without a Body*, bodies have been stripped of their capacity to signify or make sense. Instead, they embody the very violence of being stripped of that capacity: writhing in supine form, limping restlessly to a soundtrack of barking dogs (an echo, perhaps, of Prospero's order that Trinculo, Stephano and Caliban be hunted by hounds [4.1.255]), daubed from head to foot in metallic paint. Throughout the performance, whose lighting is maintained at a sepulchral dimness, anonymous robot-like bodies also speed onto the stage, slapping their thighs and chests in rapid, ritualistic fashion. Their fleet-footed, automaton-like movements suggest a mechanized

---

[69] Benjamin, *Illuminations*, p. 254.

life — are they bureaucratic enforcers, or victims of technocratic power? But these bodies too are made to disappear from visibility and signification. Hence, perhaps, the title: *Tempest without a Body*.

Yet the dream of Paradise is one that *Tempest without a Body* finds hard to give up. Much of the piece, admittedly, is hard to read. What is the Paradise from which its angel has been blown, and why do we hear a muezzin's call to prayer at the commencement of its tempest? Is the muezzin's a voice of Paradise, or is it part of the discordant clamour that constitutes the storm of history? Yet Paradise returns in far less equivocal form later in the performance. *Tempest without a Body* stages a counterpart to Caliban, originally created for the Maori activist Tame Iti. A man wearing full *moko* — or facial tattoo — and a three-piece suit comes on stage and delivers, in Maori, a blistering speech written by Iti against the decimation of his land by the Christian invaders, in which he demands a return to "the ancient life principle" of Iti's tribe or *iwi*, the native Ngai Tuhoe people.[70] Yet does *Tempest without a Body* really believe that a marvellous repossession of this "ancient life principle" is possible, especially when its tattooed Caliban is dressed in a three-piece suit — and when its explicit conceptual apparatus is indebted as much to Agamben and Benjamin as it is to Tame Iti and the Ngai Tuhoe? It would seem so. In a post-performance interview, Ponifasio suggested that *The Tempest* continues to be a powerful narrative resource for him precisely because it imagines "justice as a restoration . . . we have to go back to how things were before everything went wrong."[71] Even if the restoration imagined by *The Tempest* is mostly that of the European colonizer-figure to his home country, Ponifasio clearly sees the antidote to European colonial oppression — and American neo-colonial imperialism — as another, subaltern, restoration modelled on Prospero's.

---

[70] *Tempest without a Body*, MAU Company, program note, Dartmouth College, Hanover, NH, April 16, 2010.

[71] Lemi Ponifasio, public remarks, Dartmouth College, Hanover, NH, April 16, 2010.

Thus for all its heterodox subversiveness, and for all the pressure it would seem to place on Paradise as the bi-temporal name for both the perfect past and the redeemed future, *Tempest without a Body* still dreams of marvellous repossession. The justice it imagines, therefore, differs somewhat from that imagined by Benjamin. It does not aspire to the "weak messianic power" to redeem the invisible victims of past oppression; what it longs for, rather, is an altogether "strong" messianic power — and hence, for Benjamin, an impossible power — to fly against the storm of history and return to the Paradise from which one has been blown. *Tempest without a Body* thus glides in the global jetstream of the other anti-colonial reimaginings of *The Tempest* that I have cited above, all of which transpose the urgent demand for justice into a more dubious dream of restoration. Ponifasio's remarks about *The Tempest* are, I think, an astute reading of the play. But I am not sure they make for an astute, let alone radical, politics. How much are his and other anti-colonial reimaginings of *The Tempest* in thrall to the seductions of Caliban's dream, which is to say Prospero's and Shakespeare's culture's dream, of the desire to move forward to a brave new world by returning to something original, something whole that has been lost? How much do we really dream against the grain of *The Tempest* when we dream of marvellous repossession?

Jonathan Gil Harris is Professor of English at George Washington University, where he has taught since 2003. Prior to that, he held positions at Ithaca College, New York, and the University of Auckland in New Zealand. The past recipient of fellowships from the Folger Shakespeare Library, the Society for the Humanities at Cornell University, and the National Endowment for the Humanities, he has also served as Associate Editor of *Shakespeare Quarterly* since 2005.

Professor Harris is the author of four books: *Foreign Bodies and the Body Politic: Discourses of Social Pathology in Early Modern England* (Cambridge University Press, 1998); *Sick Economies: Drama, Mercantilism, and Disease in Shakespeare's England* (University of Pennsylvania Press, 2004); *Untimely Matter in the Time of Shakespeare* (University of Pennsylvania Press, 2008, named by *Choice* magazine as an Outstanding Academic Title for 2009); and *Shakespeare and Literary Theory* (Oxford University Press, 2010). He coedited, with Natasha Korda, *Staged Properties in Early Modern English Drama* (Cambridge University Press, 2002). He is also the editor of the third New Mermaids edition of Thomas Dekker's *The Shoemaker's Holiday* (Methuen, 2008); *Placing Michael Neill: Issues of Place in Shakespeare and Early Modern Drama* (Ashgate Press, 2011); and *Indography: Writing the "Indian" in Early Modern England* (Palgrave Macmillan, forthcoming 2012).

His 2011 Garnett Sedgewick lecture emerges from a graduate seminar he taught in 2010, called "Becoming Indian," which considered (amongst other topics) the persistence of the figure of Paradise in early modern writing about both the Americas and the orient. He is currently at work on a book project, also called *Becoming Indian*, which considers poor European travellers to India — servants, soldiers, masterless men — who to lesser and greater extents became Indian, and whose elusive lives suggest the outlines of alternate Indo-European histories that potentially unsettle modern conceptions of bodies, race, and foreignness.